De
access st
explained

URBAN
DESIGN
GROUP

Published by Thomas Telford Publishing, Thomas Telford Ltd, 1 Heron Quay, London E14 4JD.
www.thomastelford.com

Distributors for Thomas Telford books are
USA: ASCE Press, 1801 Alexander Bell Drive, Reston, VA 20191-4400, USA
Japan: Maruzen Co. Ltd, Book Department, 3–10 Nihonbashi 2-chome, Chuo-ku, Tokyo 103
Australia: DA Books and Journals, 648 Whitehorse Road, Mitcham 3132, Victoria

First published 2008

Editor

Rob Cowan, Urban Design Group and Urban Design Skills

Editorial team

Gill Butter, New Forest District Council

Flick Harris, Manchester Disabled People's Access Group

Paul Grover, Solent Centre for Architecture and Design

Bettina Kirkham, Kirkham Landscape Planning Consultants

Richard Payne, New Forest District Council

Brian Quinn, Urban Design Group

Neil Williamson, New Forest District Council and the Landscape Institute

Maya Yamashita-Shcherbakova, Urban Design Group

Cartoons by Rob Cowan

This guide is endorsed by the Landscape Institute

A catalogue record for this book is available from the British Library

ISBN: 978-0-7277-3440-2

Designed and typeset by Kneath Associates, Swansea

Printed and bound in Great Britain by Latimer Trend and Company Ltd., Plymouth

Sponsored by

planit

Planit ie is a dynamic design practice with an ability to operate on all levels of the design spectrum, from regional and city wide strategies, visionary masterplanning of urban quarters and sites, through to on-site design specification and implementation. More often than not, our services are retained from strategy to delivery. Our practice is at the vanguard of the sustainable communities agenda, and whether we are leading the design process, or working as part of a multi-disciplinary team, our philosophy is to add value. Within Planit ie there is considerable experience of all facets of design and planning, including landscape planning and environmental impact assessment; masterplanning and urban design; public inquiry and expert witness; and contract administration and project management. With 21 landscape architects and urban designers, Planit ie is the largest dedicated team in the north west. However, we believe in relationship building, and who you see is who you get.

Contact: Peter Swift, Planit ie, 10 Cecil Road, Hale, Cheshire WA15 9PA. Tel: 0161 928 9281. Fax: 0161 929 9284. www.planit-ie.com

savills

Savills Urban Design is an innovative and highly experienced team of urban design and masterplanning professionals forming part of one of the leading planning consultancies and property advisors on the international stage. Our urban design and landscape consultancy includes experts from a range of backgrounds including CABE, architecture, planning, landscape, conservation, and visual and graphic design. From the initial evaluation of the site, through public engagement, design concept, masterplanning, codes and detailed design concepts, Savills has vast experience of delivering commercially informed, but also environmentally sensitive and attractively designed places and spaces. Our design approach draws upon the expertise of Savills, most notably in research in establishing value through place making. One of the great strengths of the team approach in Savills is the continued liaison throughout the process, ensuring a streamlined and consistent strategy, and the design of deliverable and sustainable places.

Contact: Ben van Bruggen, Savills (incorporating Hepher Dixon), 1st Floor, Lansdowne House, 57 Berkeley Square, London W1J 6ER. Tel: 0203 320 8287. Mob: 0780 799 9233. bvanbruggen@savills.com

RPS

The need for development and renewal, together with the economic growth ambitions of developers, must be set against the environmental and climate change issues. New development should enrich the qualities of existing places. This means encouraging a distinctive response that arises from and complements its setting. This applies at every scale: the region, the city, the town, the neighbourhood and the street. RPS is a multidisciplinary consultancy able to draw together, in different combinations, the three related disciplines of urban design, planning and environment. As part of our inclusive and high quality service to our clients, RPS has been producing design and access statements in support of planning applications, which have now become mandatory for all but the smallest of developments. Each statement is individually tailored to the requirements of the project to ensure that the relevant authorities and community are provided with the appropriate information to make informed and balanced decisions.

RPS, Salisbury House, Tettenhall Road, Wolverhampton WV1 4SG. Tel: 01902 771331. www.rpsgroup.com/urbandesign

taylor young|ty

Taylor Young is a recognised market leader in urban design, masterplanning, planning, architecture and landscape architecture, with commissions in the sectors of commercial, residential, education, healthcare, public services, area regeneration and design guidance. With over 150 staff based in Manchester, Liverpool and Cheshire, we combine creative and visionary design with practical planning advice and pragmatic delivery across wide-ranging development and regeneration projects for public and private sector clients. We are committed to placemaking, and introduced our clients to design and access statements before they became a statutory requirement, demonstrating their usefulness in a wide range of successful planning applications.

Contact: Lesley Gleave, Taylor Young, Chadsworth House, Wilmslow Road, Handforth, Cheshire SK9 3HP. Tel: 01625 542 200. Fax: 01625 542 250. www.tayloryoung.co.uk

Terence O'Rourke

creating successful environments

At Terence O'Rourke we are dedicated to creating successful environments and to making good projects happen. We specialise in town planning, urban design, environmental consultancy, landscape architecture, architecture and graphic design. A key strength of our approach is the close integration of these disciplines, enabling us to provide comprehensive, innovative solutions to a range of planning, masterplanning, environmental and design challenges. Our public and private sector projects include housing, regeneration, education, commercial, transport, leisure and tourism, utilities, renewable energy and waste schemes. We operate throughout the UK, with more than 120 staff at offices in Bournemouth, Bath and Edinburgh.

Terence O'Rourke, Everdene House, Deansleigh Road, Bournemouth BH7 7DU. Tel: 01202 421142. Fax: 01202 430055. maildesk@torltd.co.uk www.torltd.co.uk

3

Design and access statements explained

'The test of a design statement is not how much it weighs or how glossy it is, but how well it communicates. If the applicant can tell the story in a few pages, that's long enough for me'

Development control planner, north east England

Contents

Acknowledgements

Thanks are due to Scott Adams, David Chapman, Esther Kurland, Barry Sellers and Matthew White for their comments on earlier drafts.

Manchester Disabled People's Access Group

Manchester Disabled People's Access Group (MDPAG) has advised on access issues in this guide, though it is not responsible for the final text.

MDPAG is an organisation of disabled people, specialising in access consultancy, access audits, training, publications and the development of best practice design. With ten years' experience of working with planning authorities, it provides consultancy for a range of large and small projects in a number of sectors, including PFI schemes. MDPAG can also advise on consulting with disabled people.

Information and advice available from MDPAG includes templates, checklists and best practice standards to help in the preparation and delivery of design and access statements, particularly on access for disabled people. The group can also advise on legislation and guidance, including the Disability Discrimination Act, planning guidance and building regulations, and their effect on designs and decision making.

Contact: Manchester Disabled People's Access Group, Business Employment Venture Centre, Aked Close, Ardwick, Manchester M12 4AN. admin@mdpag.org.uk; tel: 0161 273 5033; www.mdpag.org.uk

This guide in no way purports to be either exclusive or exhaustive. The Urban Design Group does not accept liability for any action arising from the use to which it may be put.

The guide applies specifically to England and Wales.

The Urban Design Group, founded in 1978, is a membership organisation whose aim is to promote effective action in improving towns and cities. See page 73 for details of the group and how to join.

Foreword

What is or is not a design and access statement is a rather different question to what makes a good one.

In August 2006, the Government had high aspirations for raising the design standard of what is built. Baroness Andrews announced that 'the Government is putting high-quality design at the heart of the planning process'.

Design and access statements have become the most important interface between local authorities and planning applicants. The design and access statement has become the most prominent of all the application documents. It is the one most commonly read by professionals and often the only one read by everyone else.

Surprisingly, then, the standard of practice is still generally low and there is a great deal of confusion. The quality of the statements and local authorities' skill in using and interpreting them will help to determine the quality of design.

The UDG's new publication follows its previous guides *Urban Design Guidance: urban design frameworks, development briefs and master plans* and *Graphics for Urban Design*, both also published by Thomas Telford. These two UDG guides have been credited with significantly improving standards of practice and are regularly quoted in articles on these subjects.

This publication is not another 'how to' guide (we have plenty of these already), but rather a 'how to do better' guide. It will be invaluable to applicants, their design teams and local authority planners unfamiliar with design development and the tools of urban design. Rob Cowan and his team have put together a first-rate publication that will find its home within easy reach on the desk rather than tucked away on the shelf.

Ben van Bruggen

Chairman
Urban Design Group

Ten pointers to good practice

1. Children doing maths homework are told: 'Show your thinking!' The message to people producing design statements is the same.

2. A developer should prepare a design statement as part of the pre-application process, rather than getting a consultant to prepare it in isolation.

3. Far too many design statements are post-rationalisations, with developers trying to justify predetermined designs. The time to start writing the design statement is at the start of the process.

4. A design statement should be part of an audit trail of the design and approval process. Using design statements involves a different approach to the process of design, rather than being just a matter of cobbling together a document at the end.

5. Think of the design statement as a process, not a product.

6. Most design statements are far too long. Sometimes this is a deliberate ploy to swamp the planners with information. In other cases it is just that the applicant has not thought about what aspects of the development are most important. Anyone writing a design statement should ask: 'how little can we say to explain the important points about this scheme?' Some design statements, on the other hand, are too short: their authors just go through the motions, using the standard headings but failing to explain their thinking.

HMM... IT LOOKS LIKE I'LL HAVE TO VISIT THE SITE.

Using design statements involves a different approach to the process of design.

7. Design statements should be read, not weighed.

8. Every picture tells a story. To convey what that story is almost always needs the picture to have a caption or to be annotated. Do not use pictures or drawings merely as wallpaper. Say either: 'this picture is a small version of the one in the planning application' or 'this is illustrative only, and similar to what is proposed'. The design statement is in support of the planning application, but not for determination, and must have that cross-referencing.

9. Most urban design follows one of the currently orthodox new urban forms: instead of considering what is appropriate for the particular site and area, the designer designs as though with a rubber stamp. A design statement should expose such lack of thinking.

10. A good design statement cannot justify a poor design.

Ten common defects of design statements

1. Including matters that are not relevant to the planning decision.

2. Regurgitating planning policies and design guidance.

3. Describing, without explaining the reasons for the design choices.

4. Failing to provide a rationale explaining how the analysis of the context led to the chosen design principles.

5. Paying lip service to or ignoring inclusive design issues, and showing a lack of understanding of people with special access needs.

6. Too much detail and technical information, and writing in jargon.

7. Repeating what is in the drawings.

8. Irrelevant or poorly presented illustrations.

9. Merely reproducing the developer's marketing material.

10. Treating access as a separate matter or producing two statements when one is required.

Part One
What is a design statement for?

Who this guide is for

This guide is for developers and local authority planners who want to achieve a high standard of development. It will be helpful even where a design statement is not obligatory.

Who this guide is not for

This guide is not for developers who believe that hiring expensive lawyers is a better way of getting their proposals through the planning system than insisting on good design, or for local authorities for whom effective communication with planning applicants is not a priority.

The purpose of this guide

This guide is intended for people who are submitting design statements, receiving them, negotiating on them, being consulted on them, or providing local guidance on them. That includes developers and their agents, planners, urban designers, architects, planning lawyers, councillors, access groups and members of local communities. The guide explains what design statements are for, how to go about preparing one and how to use them.

This guide aims to encourage good practice and innovation rather than prescribe a standardised tick-box approach. Design statements must be relevant and specific to the site in question and must not merely collate together bland, generic commentary or regurgitate existing published guidance. Councils themselves should tailor their own local guidance to the particular place and their own policies, and planning applicants should root their proposals – and their explanations of them – in a full understanding of the local context.

The requirement for design statements

Design statements are required by the Planning and Compulsory Purchase Act 2004.

Section 42(1) of that Act introduced an amendment to section 62 of the Town and Country Planning Act 1990, requiring the submission of a design statement; and section 42(5) prevents local planning authorities from entertaining an application which is not accompanied by a design statement (subject to some exceptions set out below).

Governments guidance on design statements is set out in Department for Communities and Local Government (DCLG) Circular 01/2006: *Guidance on Changes to the Development Control System* (www.communities.gov.uk/documents/ planningandbuilding/pdf/144854), paragraphs 56 to 110. This refers to them as 'design and access statements' (to encourage the integration of design and access principles in approaches to design). Some limited guidance has been provided by CABE (Commission for Architecture and the Built Environment) in *Design and Access Statements: how to read, write and use them* (2006, revised edition in 2007). This present document is consistent with the DCLG's and CABE's guidance, but we hope to help users to get more out of the potential of design statements.

The Disability Discrimination Act (DDA) requires buildings used by the public to be accessible to disabled people, and requires employers to make reasonable adjustments to their buildings for individual employees. It requires providers of services to anticipate the needs of disabled people, who can take legal action if the physical or other barriers are unreasonable. The DDA does not refer to any specifications. It is fair to assume that what is 'reasonable' will be defined more precisely over time. Using best practice standards wherever possible should provide a level of protection under the law for developers and building managers, ensuring that disabled people are not excluded from new buildings and environments.

The DDA may also override Part M of the Building Regulations (and Part B in certain circumstances, particularly in design elements which are not covered by Part M).

What is a design statement?

A design statement is a written and illustrated report, which accompanies a planning application. The statement shows how the applicant has analysed the site and its setting, and formulated and applied design principles to achieve good, inclusive design for buildings and public spaces; and how the developer or designer has consulted or will consult on the issues. The statement's scope and level of detail are determined by the nature of the development, the site and its context. The statement has a specific job to do in explaining the background thinking that led to the planning proposal being drawn up. It is not just a description of the planning proposal.

When does a planning applicant have to submit a design statement?

We should expect a high standard of design for every planning application, and a design statement will almost always be useful. Some local authorities may require a design statement for all applications other than for domestic buildings, although the government's regulations do not go quite so far as that.

The government specifies that a design statement is required for any planning application except for:

- a material change in the use of land or buildings (unless it also involves operational development)

- engineering or mining operations

- the development of an existing dwelling house (except in a designated area: a national park, site of special scientific interest, conservation area, area of outstanding natural beauty, world heritage site or the Broads).

A design statement is not required for an application relating to advertisement control, a tree preservation order or the storage of hazardous substances.

13

Applicants should contact the local authority as early as possible for advice about the level of detail needed. For all major schemes, applicants should enter into pre-application discussions, and in some cases it will be appropriate to submit a draft design statement at this stage. Drawings, diagrams, plans and preliminary design statements will provide the basis for fruitful discussion.

In the case of an outline planning permission, the applicant and the local planning authority should think about how they will make sure that the relevant parts of the statement are kept to when future details are being drawn up or assessed, and that they are passed on at building control stage. This may be the stage when the planners are considering an application for the approval of reserved matters or any matter reserved by condition, such as materials or landscape details.

It will be particularly important that the statement's principles are 'fixed' (to use the official word) in the interests of future decisions. This means that the applicant will need to make clear in the design statement which elements of it are to be fixed, and also ensure that they are specific and measurable enough to allow compliance to be checked in future. Local planning authorities should impose planning conditions to make sure this happens. Otherwise the principles will not be binding.

At the reserved matters stage, the local planning authority may feel that additional information, building on the original statement, is required. If so, it should consider setting out such a requirement through a condition on the outline planning permission.

If a design statement is required, a local authority should not register a planning application until one has been submitted.

Design statements at pre-application stage

A developer can open the dialogue with a draft design statement to explain the conclusions of the context appraisals and the design principles on which a development proposal in progress is based. This enables the local authority to give an initial response to the main issues raised by the proposal. A draft at this stage can be less detailed, looser and freer than the design statement that will later be submitted with a planning application for either outline or full planning permission. A draft design statement should be a living document that provides a sound basis for good communications.

It will often be appropriate for applicants to consult independently on access issues and not just to rely on the consultation process undertaken by the planning authority. Consulting access groups and using access consultants can save time and money by identifying any access barriers and solutions at an early stage.

The role of a design statement

A design statement forms part of the planning application in support of the development proposed, but is not for determination in the same way that the application drawings are, for example. This allows applicants to express ideas without being bound by the requirements of approval. The local planning authority can grant planning permission with conditions. Those conditions can be linked to elements in the design statement, in much the same way as a condition can refer to a letter written by the applicant agreeing to, for example, use a certain building material.

In a case where the applicant submits a new scheme, minor alterations or reserved matters, the local authority can request a statement of conformity. This will confirm that these new matters follow the principles set out in the original design statement.

Designing for inclusion

Buildings and environments often have physical and sensory barriers that make it difficult or impossible for disabled people and others with special access needs to use the space. Minimum and best practice standards are intended to allow these people to use buildings and the environments safely and independently. Such standards will relate to some of the barriers experienced by people with physical, sensory or neuro-diverse impairments, and by learning-disabled people.

Specific and specialist areas in buildings and environments are not always covered by standards, or the standards may be out of date. This is where early consultation with disabled people's organisations, access groups and users can be helpful and save money at a later stage. Inclusive design need not be seen as a bar to imaginative and effective designs. Design statements can provide a way of involving potential users as well as the designers, engineers and other consultants.

Some developments involve a number of contractors and sometimes require consultations with organisations responsible for site facilities and land or transport, other than the client. Consulting with these bodies, as part of the design statement process, using principles 'fixed' with the planning authority, can go some way to ensuring that all parties involved in developments are working to the same best practice access standards. It should help to avoid some parties creating access barriers to parts of the environment.

There is no legal requirement to include internal specifications in a design statement, although they will be required later at building control/approved inspector stage. However, it is very helpful to have an understanding of the access barriers and solutions and best practice standards within a building as well as in the external environment. This can help ensure that the overall size, layout, emergency evacuation plans and general design will meet the minimum (and, where possible, the best practice) specifications.

15

Design statements for full planning applications

Whereas much of the detail of an outline proposal can be worked up later under reserved matters (guided by the approved design statement), this option is not available for a full application. Here a great deal more certainty is required, and only more minor or very detailed matters are reserved for approval under condition. A full application must show, through its design statement and other documentation, that the proposal is achievable, and meets current inclusive design standards and requirements (for some local authorities, this will include best practice access standards in the local development framework).

Planning conditions

The local planning authority can grant permission subject to conditions. A good design statement can provide the basis for setting such conditions. It can relate to matters that are set out in the design statement, such as the parameters for the height of the building (in the case of an outline application) or width of streets, for example. But the authority cannot impose a condition requiring the scheme to be built in accordance with the whole design statement as this would be too uncertain and so impossible to enforce.

The authority will impose conditions in the light of its view as to which aspects of the design are most important. The applicant may appeal against a condition if he or she finds it unacceptable, or the applicant can apply to vary the condition if unforeseen circumstances cause the proposed development to be altered. Planning conditions always have to pass the six-fold test of being: necessary; relevant to planning; relevant to the development; enforceable; precise; and reasonable in all other respects.

16

Raising standards of inclusive design

Design statements are an important means of raising standards of design in new development. They can have important benefits for all stakeholders, particularly in promoting effective communication between all the parties involved.

- For *developers and building managers*, good design statements can reduce conflict, speed up decision-making in the planning process, encourage better relationships with local communities and other organisations, increase certainty of outcomes, and enhance a developer's reputation for good design. The design statement can also document the commitment to good access for disabled people under the DDA. The design statement should be seen as a positive part of the design process rather than as a cost to be minimised and resented. When the statement is continued through building control approval to building management, as advised by the Disability Rights Commission, it can be updated on a regular basis.

- For *architects and urban designers*, the process of developing a design statement can help a design team explain the rationale behind its design proposal to the client/developer, and develop convincing arguments to use in negotiation with planning authorities. It can also provide the basis for the access statements required by Part M of the building regulations.

- For *local authorities*, good design statements can provide a structure and focus to negotiations, and can document the negotiations' evolution. They can provide a framework to allow planners to defend their requirements robustly, and seek specific clarification and improvements.

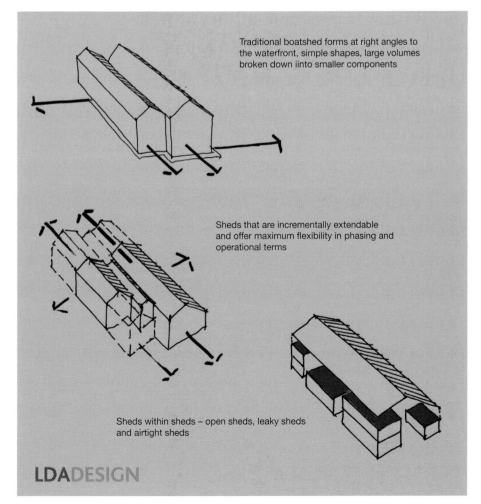

Traditional boatshed forms at right angles to the waterfront, simple shapes, large volumes broken down iinto smaller components

Sheds that are incrementally extendable and offer maximum flexibility in phasing and operational terms

Sheds within sheds – open sheds, leaky sheds and airtight sheds

Using traditional building forms as the basis for new development: sketches from LDA Design's design statement for East Cowes.

LDADESIGN

17

■ For *local communities*, a developer's design statement can help to structure and record local consultation, and make sure that development proposals are clearly explained.

The best statements set out their analysis, principles, concepts and decision-making processes briefly and cogently, keeping readers interested and focusing on the main issues that are relevant to the site.

The requirement to produce a design statement should not be onerous, although it will depend on good design skills. The statement should formalise the work and process that a good designer and actively involved client will be doing anyway.

Good design should be the aim of all involved in the development process and should be encouraged everywhere. Government advice in *Planning Policy Statement 1* (PPS1) sets out the requirements for good design in development proposals. The Department for Communities and Local Government, and Commission for Architecture and the Built Environment (CLG/CABE) guidance – *By Design: Urban design in the planning system: towards better practice* – sets out advice on how to achieve better design solutions. In setting out principles, each of these guides explains that successful design depends on interpreting them in the context of the site.

> 'Good design ensures attractive usable, durable and adaptable places and is a key element in achieving sustainable development. Good design is indivisible from good planning … Design which is inappropriate in its context, or which fails to take the opportunities available for improving the character and quality of an area and the way it functions, should not be accepted.' *Planning Policy Statement 1: Delivering Sustainable Development*

Why does this guide use the term 'design statements' and not 'design and access statements'?

'Design and access statement' is a term introduced by the government regulations. Previously there were design statements and, in the case of some developments where a special focus on access was thought necessary, separate access statements. The government regulations insist that the newly required statements will be called 'design and access statements'.

The government's intention is to make clear that access will be fully considered in the new generation of statements. But the joint term is confusing.

Access is a major element of the design of buildings and places. 'Design' and 'access' are not just two aspects of development: design is a process, and good access is one of the important qualities that design should achieve. Access is fundamental to how all people use all places. Two of the seven 'objectives of urban design' that are at the heart of the CLG/ CABE guide *By Design* (which sets out how design should be handled by the planning system) are 'Quality of the public realm: To promote public space and routes that are attractive, safe, uncluttered and work effectively for all in society, including disabled and elderly people' and 'Ease of movement: To promote accessibility ...'

Calling the statements 'design and access statements' suggests that design and access are two distinct subjects, which they are not. It would be just as illogical to refer to 'design and sustainability statements', or 'design and community safety statements', as these are also among the government's fundamental objectives for design. Picking any of them for separate mention in the title would suggest that they are issues that can be tackled through the planning system separately from design. For that reason, this guide refers to 'design statements', as we hope that in due course that will be how they are known. For the moment, many people who use the statements will use the government's phrase 'design and access statement', to indicate that they are following the regulations. We have titled this guide *Design and Access Statements* to make it clear to potential readers that we and the government are talking about the same documents.

It is important, of course, that the essential role of access in design should be very strongly stressed. Too often in the past it has not been, or it has been considered as little more than an added extra. Integrating access into design statements – in name and deed – should make the access element stronger, not weaker.

Should design statements be required for change of use or householder applications?

The government's regulations do not require design statements to be submitted with change of use applications. Nevertheless, local authorities may well wish to encourage applicants to submit a design statement in such circumstances, and applicants may welcome the chance to explain their proposals. Access statements are required at building control approval stage for change of use, so it can be helpful to start the process at planning approval stage.

Nor do the government regulations require a householder application (for the development of an existing dwelling house) to be accompanied by a design statement, unless the house is in a designated area. This exclusion also seems unjustified. First, the cumulative effect of minor development has a major impact on the environment. Second, it is illogical for there to be a cut-off point in terms of size. The important point is that a design statement should be appropriate to the size and complexity of the development. The statement for a small, simple scheme – a householder application, for example – might fit on one page, yet still be of value in explaining the thinking behind the design. (Where adaptations are carried out to meet the specific requirements of a resident, it may be appropriate to diverge from some of the best practice standards designed to cover the maximum number of disabled people. A design statement would explain the reasons behind the proposals.)

It is not as though the applicant is being asked to carry out design processes that could be avoided without a design statement. Appraisal of the development's context is essential whatever the scale of the development, so the statement does not require an appraisal that would otherwise not need to have been carried out. Similarly, the design principles that need to be set out in the statement are an essential stage of the design process for any development that will reach the necessary standard of design.

The design of housing should take account of the requirements of disabled people and large families of all ages. The use of standards such as Lifetime Homes and the Code for Sustainable Homes, and the more inclusive standards of Manchester City Council's *Design for Access 2* manual, for example, have been shown to make the houses more attractive to users. Planning authorities may decide to ensure that all or some of the new housing developments meet more inclusive standards.

Engineering and mining works

There is no requirement to submit a design statement to support an application for engineering and mining works. Such works do have a design component, though, and they often require the submission of a planning statement, an environmental statement or environmental impact analysis. The process of producing a design statement will have considerable benefit here too. It will set out an approach to assessing local context, and show how the design and phasing of development, the management of the site and environmental mitigation measures have responded to that context.

Design statements for outline planning applications

The Planning and Compulsory Purchase Act 2004 makes a distinction between two types of design and access statement: one type for outline applications, and the other for full or detailed applications.

One of the government's reasons for introducing design statements was to make outline planning applications more reliable, in the face of criticism of them for being too vague. The aim was to narrow the gap between outline and detailed planning permission.

There is a danger of such applications putting local authorities in a position of feeling obliged at a later stage to approve reserved matters that it would have been unlikely to approve if they had been submitted as a detailed application in the first place. The government decided that the more general use of design statements would reduce this danger.

Principles of building form, materials and details described in the design statement for Hunts Grove, Gloucestershire by Barton Willmore.

1. Squares are to be a major feature along the primary route with strong frontage

2. Squares can contain some parking but not to the detriment of them being pedestrian zones

3. Buildings at focal points should be treated as Landmark Buildings and should be treated accordingly in their scale, materials and architectural style

4. Deviations in road path and obstrusive visitors parking can be used to aid traffic calming

5. Mews courtyards or rear parking courts enable a non car dominated frontage to be a feature of this character area

6. Roads should be designed to follow buildings

7. Buildings should front onto main cycle/pedestrian routes to ensure users are safe and secure

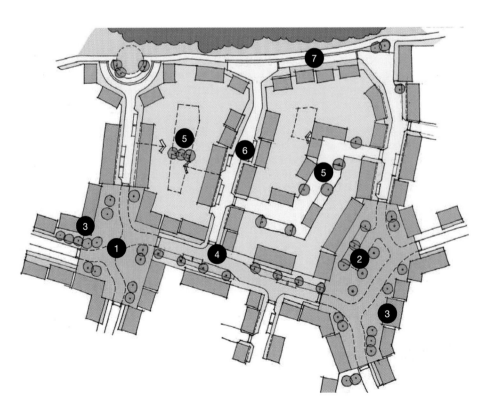

20

A design statement must accompany a planning application whether the application is for outline or full planning permission. The elements of the statement will be the same for outline or full planning permission. Only the scope of the statement will differ.

A statement accompanying an outline planning application may have less detail, but the essentials must be there. Indeed, the fact that, at outline stage, the detailed design has not been determined makes it all the more important to explain the appraisals and the design principles.

The design statement will leave room for flexibility by indicating the parameters (maximum and minimum) of possible solutions; a range of heights or densities, for example; an average height or density for the site as a whole; or a range of minimum heights and densities for parts of the site.

The design statement will be a material consideration in determining a planning application for approval of reserved matters.

Local planning authorities should draw up local development framework policies setting out the information to be submitted in a design statement and explaining how the council will relate that information to the planning approval, for example through conditions. A legal agreement is likely to be appropriate for a large or complex scheme.

It will be particularly important that the statement's key principles are 'fixed' (to use the official word) in the interests of future decisions. The statement is fixed when the local authority imposes planning conditions which restrict the scope of reserved matters by reference to the contents of the design statement. On this basis, amendments can be made to the design, and additional information provided without compromising the agreed outline design principles. This highlights the need to ensure that design principles agreed at outline stage are achievable, and that potential conflicts of interest have been properly examined.

A design statement can highlight problems early in the planning process.

21

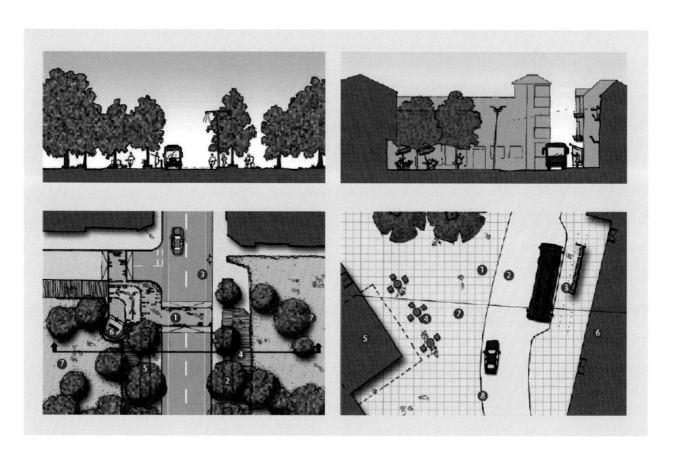

Proposed street types illustrated in the design statement for Great Western Park, Didcot, by PRP Landscape and Urban for Taylor Woodrow/Wimpey Strategic.

How does a design statement help local authorities, planning applicants and other stakeholders?

Preparing a design statement will help with processing the application. It can:

- Help to promote constructive pre-application discussions, highlighting any problems or queries early in the planning process.

- Help to speed up the decision-making process by explaining the applicant's thinking to planners and local communities.

- Demonstrate how the context (economic and social as well as physical) has been properly examined at the relevant scale for the site, and how the design has been developed in response to this.

- Help applicants to identify their design obligations and needs early on, to take on and retain the necessary design expertise throughout (including access consultations and specialists where appropriate), and to use a rigorous design method.

- Act as a documentary record of the design process, telling a clear story about the site and the proposals (including ways of overcoming barriers to access), and how the local community has responded.

- Demonstrate how the various aspects of the design process (including access, resource use, environmental impact, transport and community safety) have been brought together from the early stages.

22

Preparing a design statement will help to achieve better development. It can:

- Ensure that inclusive design is properly considered from the very start of the project.

- Encourage developers to be more aware of the potential of good inclusive design.

- Help to enhance the local sense of place, and the positive qualities of the local landscape and townscape.

- Help attract business and investment.

- Require designers to provide evidence and justification for a scheme that may challenge planners.

- Make it easier for local communities to understand the planning process and to get actively involved in it.

- Educate and inform the wider public, including business and residential communities, of the potential benefits of high-quality new development.

- Reduce conflict between disparate interests, resulting in better all-round solutions and avoiding last-minute design compromises.

Part Two
Writing a design statement

What is required for a design statement?

A design statement should explain the design principles and concepts that have been applied to particular aspects of the proposal. The government's circular defines these as the amount, layout, scale, landscaping and appearance of the development.

Use

What the development will be used for. This may also include how the development will improve access to facilities.

Amount

The amount of development is how much development is proposed (the number of proposed units in the case of residential use or, for all other development, the proposed floor space for each proposed use).

It would be helpful to be clear about the space required for compliance with Part M standards and evacuation proposals, as a minimum, and, where possible, to best practice standards – taking account of such matters as accessible toilet design, evacuation lifts, circulation space around fixtures and fittings, and width of corridors and stairways.

The design statement should explain why the density of the proposed scheme is justified, not just in light of policy targets, but in response to the local context.
Photo: Urban Design Skills

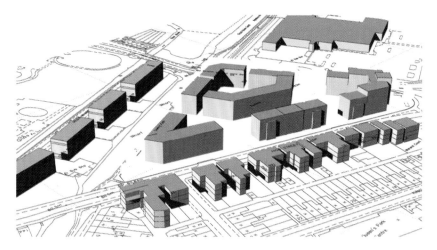

A representation of massing for a proposal by RPS

The amount cannot be reserved within an outline application. But it is common to express a maximum amount of floorspace for each use, and for this to be made the subject of a planning condition.

Layout

The layout is the way in which buildings, routes and open spaces (both private and public) are provided and placed in relation to each other and buildings and spaces surrounding the development.

Access considerations could include ease of orientation, unobstructed and logical routes, clear evacuation and access to transport, and accessible parking and drop-off. The design statement should include the area, or areas, for each access point to the development, including connections with the surrounding network, circulation within a site, suitability of public and other transport links including travel distances, means of escape, and how inclusive access will be ensured.

If layout is reserved at the outline stage, the outline planning application should provide information on the approximate location of buildings, routes and open spaces proposed.

Liverpool's city centre model helps local people understand the scale and context of development. Photo: Urban Design Skills

27

Scale

Scale is the height, width and length of a building in relation to its surroundings.

If scale has been reserved at the outline stage, the application should still indicate upper and lower limits of the height, width and length of each building.

Landscaping

Landscape design is the treatment of private and public spaces to enhance or protect the amenities of the site and the area.

If landscape design is reserved at the outline stage, the outline application does not need to provide any detailed landscape information.

Lack of thought about how development relates to the local landscape can lead to the creation of a place with no sense of being at all distinctive. Photo: Urban Design Skills

28

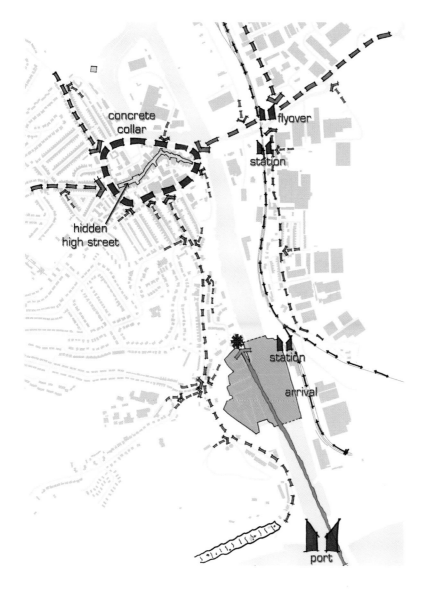

Diagram of movement and links at Newhaven Riverside by Terence O'Rourke

The concept of 'landscaping' described in the circular is fairly limited. A good design statement will go beyond it, and will probably discuss 'landscape design' rather than 'landscaping'. Landscape design uses a thorough understanding of the landscape of the site and area as the basis for developing the proposal's overall design principles. This requires consideration of spatial relationships between built and natural elements, their functions, significance and appearance, from the broad scale down to the fine detailed level. Accessibility issues will include consideration of materials used, unobstructed routes, good orientation, personal and community safety and details such as toilet areas for assistance dogs (mainly for public buildings).

Appearance

Appearance is what a development looks like. This is determined by the external built form of the development, its architecture, materials, decoration, lighting, colour, texture and boundary treatments.

Some materials will be hazardous or obstructions for disabled people, but good design will be helpful for all users of the building or environment.

29

A development in central Glasgow incorporates public art, introducing imaginative new forms while continuing the rhythm of the street. Photo: Urban Design Skills

If appearance is reserved at the outline stage, the outline application does not need to provide any specific information on the issue. While detail is not always needed in the outline application, some indication of expected qualities may well be needed to justify the application.

Some local planning authorities insist on the specific terms – use, amount, layout, scale, landscaping and appearance – being used to structure any design statement, so any statement should mention them prominently, and provide clear cross-referencing so that a reader can find the relevant information in the design statement (particularly in the section on design principles). In assessing a design statement, a local authority should not assume that it is a good one just because the specified headings are used, or that it is necessarily defective if they are not used.

Emerging guidance

Particular cases will continue to shed new light on what is required from a design statement. An example is the refusal by the secretary of state, in 2007, of a planning appeal by Bovis Homes and BAE Systems. The case concerned the development of 2 200 dwellings, 66 000 sqm of employment, and other development, at Filton Airfield, Bristol.

The solicitors Addleshaw Goddard noted that this was the first significant secretary of state decision addressing the profound changes to the requirements for outline planning applications which had came into force in 2006. The decision gave clear guidance on what design statements, design codes and masterplans must include for an outline permission to be granted.

The secretary of state, in endorsing the advice of the planning inspector, confirmed that a design statement should explain and justify the principles behind the choice between development zones and blocks or building plots, and explain how the principles would inform the detailed layout. It was no longer appropriate for a design statement to include a small number of worked examples of perimeter blocks or similar broad indications of development parcels, with no clear indication of their built form.

In particular, sample block layouts would need to be much more than watercolour-type graphic interpretations. These, the secretary of state noted, could be difficult to interpret, lacking detail and precision. Any cross-sections would need to be sufficiently plentiful and accurate to provide a clear understanding of the three-dimensional form.

Addleshaw Goddard pointed out that it would now be important to demonstrate how principles, set out in the text of a design statement, might be applied in practice. The secretary of state required worked-up examples showing building heights, the distribution between flats and houses, the allocation of parking spaces and garages, public and private spaces, and similar matters.

Combined statements

Where a planning application is submitted in parallel with an application for listed building consent, a single, combined statement should be provided. Alongside the requirements for all planning applications, the statement should include information on the historical and architectural importance of the building; the specific physical features that justify its designation as a listed building; the building's setting; how any design has an impact on these features; why this is necessary; and what measures have been taken to minimise such impact. This will include any access features. Listed building status does not negate the requirement under the DDA and Part M to ensure that access is improved.

Explaining the design

The content of a design statement will reflect the scale, type and complexity of the proposals. But in all cases the design statement's objective will be the same: to explain a design based on thorough analysis of the context and a clear design process.

31

The best solution for one site is unlikely to be appropriate elsewhere. Each site must be considered on its own merits.

A design must evolve from an evaluation of the site and its context, a process that will often involve the local community. The design will be based on an understanding of the qualities that we expect from a successful place. The CLG/CABE guidance, *By Design*, identifies the following qualities as the 'objectives of urban design':

- Character (the identity of the place).

- Continuity and enclosure (how public and private space will be clearly distinguished from one another).

- Convivial public realm (how public spaces and routes can be made lively and pleasant to use).

- Ease of movement (how the place can be made easy to get to and move through).

- Legibility (how the place can have a clear image and be easy to understand).

- Adaptability (how the place can change easily).

- Diversity and choice (how the place can provide variety and mixed uses).

Successful places must always be designed and planned with a view to how the place will integrate land use, transport and the natural environment.

Three straightforward and simple steps must be undertaken for every design statement: appraising the site and context; identifying inclusive design principles; and describing and explaining the design. The statement also explains how the three relate to one another.

Site and context appraisal

The design statement should include a factual and accurate survey and assessment of the site and its surroundings. The area to be surveyed and assessed will depend on the scale of the development and the extent of its influence. These should be discussed as part of the initial discussions. Topics to be addressed will depend on the features of the site and its surroundings, and the scale and complexity of the project.

The applicant will need to identify the character, characteristics, constraints and opportunities found within the site itself, the area surrounding the site, and a wider area that the development might influence or be influenced by.

If the developer has carried out an affordability analysis, a demographic analysis (to assess the need for schools, for example) or an access audit, these should be brought into the design process as well.

A visualisation of a proposed mix use development for St Modwen at Project Jennifer, Great Homer Street, Liverpool, by Planit ie

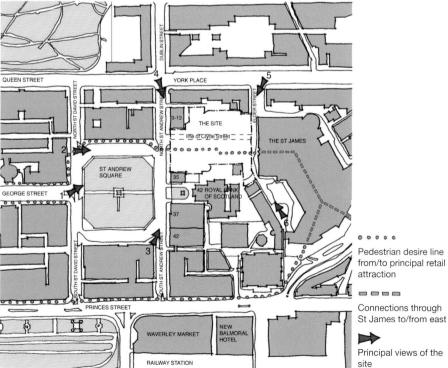

• • • • •
Pedestrian desire line from/to principal retail attraction

▬ ▬ ▬ ▬
Connections through St James to/from east

▶
Principal views of the site

Urban context diagram from the design statement for St Andrew Square, Edinburgh, by Comprehensive Design Architects for Coal Pension Properties.

A design statement will set out the findings of the appraisal of the local context. Photo: Urban Design Skills

Public involvement

Depending on the nature and scale of the development, all parts of the planning and design process may need to involve a wide range of people with an interest in the area: people who live or work there, or who own property there, or have some other interest in the place. Their views, interests and perspectives should be reflected in the appraisals, and in the process of drawing up design principles in the light of those appraisals. The design statement should explain who has been involved, in what way, what the outcome was, and how this influenced the design process.

Design principles

Drawing up a set of inclusive design principles is an essential part of the process of design development. The aim is to set out the main criteria that the design needs to achieve.

Design principles will evolve from the client's brief, the policy review, the site and context appraisal, and the designer's creativity. The principles can usefully be agreed during pre-application discussions between the applicant and council officers. These will form the basis of the design. The applicant must also show how the design principles will meet local plan policy. The final design statement should show how any conflict between the principles has been resolved in the design itself.

The design

The design process is likely to involve exploring more than one design option. Options will be tested against the project objectives and the design principles.

Local authorities will reject designs and statements where it is evident that the appraisal and design principles have merely been used to justify a predetermined design. The design solution must be clear and comprehensive, with a level of detail appropriate to the scale and complexity of the scheme.

The application of urban design
principles in Glasgow's Gorbals
district has created the qualities
of a traditional urban street.
Photo: Urban Design Skills

A design statement should explain
the thinking behind an innovative
design. Photo: Urban Design Skills

35

Access and inclusive design

A design statement, prepared in line with the government regulations, will cover those elements of access that are, in a statutory sense, relevant to the planning system. A design statement can go further than this, though, extending to other matters that have in the past been covered in separate access statements. (The Disability Rights Commission's guidance on access statements, initially developed for access statements at building control stage, may be useful: see www.drc-gb.org.) Such a design statement can provide an opportunity for developers, designers and managers of environments to demonstrate how they are meeting, or will meet, the obligations placed on them by legislation, and how they will continue to promote good accessibility through their projects.

All design statements should reflect the philosophy of 'inclusive design'. This is an evolving philosophy rather than a fixed set of design criteria. The aim of creating an inclusive environment is not to meet every need, but to remove barriers and features leading to exclusion and to maximise access for everyone. It is important not to segregate access and facilities for disabled people or see them as add-ons, but to ensure that all access is integrated into all design features.

An inclusive environment will be used easily by as many people as possible without undue effort, special treatment or separation. It will offer people the freedom to choose how they access and use it, and to participate equally in all activities that take place there. It accommodates diversity and difference (making prayer rooms and baby changing areas accessible to disabled people, for example), and it is safe, legible, predictable and logical. The aim should be to give everyone as much choice as possible in moving around on foot, wheelchair, bike, or with a buggy, and not having to rely on a car or some other means of transport. Design should ensure that there are no hazards or obstructions for people with sensory impairments.

A design statement should explain how the development will link in with the local routes and patterns of movement. Photo: Urban Design Skills

Many aspects of disabled access are covered by building control approval. But by that stage in the development process some fundamental decisions relating to accessibility, such as the orientation and location of a building, its means of access and its relation to means of transport, will have already been taken. Thus, the developer is likely to be reluctant to make major changes at this stage.

A design statement should include details of all consultations with disabled people, access consultants and user groups. Consultation (with access groups and panels, for example) should complement other professional and technical advice. Some access groups will work closely with designers to develop creative solutions to inclusive design problems. The statement should record sources of advice used for accessibility and access issues, including legislation and guidance, specialist consultants and technical advice, access audits, and surveys and consultations.

It will be particularly useful in relation to issues of accessibility if the design statement is updated as the project develops, and used as a basis for decisions by all designers and contractors. It will provide an audit trail of design decisions. After the project has been completed, the statement can be used as evidence and a record of the basis of decisions in any legal challenge under the Disability Discrimination Act.

Access issues should be considered in the light of the barriers that can be faced by people with visual impairments, hearing impairments, mobility impairments, learning difficulties, and cognitive and neuro-diverse impairments. Where barriers to access cannot be overcome, the design statement should state why it is not possible, what the implications for users are, and what other methods are being proposed.

In designing the layout of development, particular attention should be paid to circulation routes, travel distances and gradients. The siting, orientation and landscape design should consider carefully how the development can be made easily accessible, for example by providing appropriate surfaces and avoiding barriers. Careful attention should be given to seating, lighting and signage.

The design statement should deal with access to a building, and around its external spaces, but not within the building. Of course access to the building will be closely related to internal movement, so to some extent the two must be thought about together.

37

Community safety

Good planning and design have a major role to play in promoting community safety and fighting crime. Design statements should explain what consideration has been given to community safety and crime prevention. Where appropriate, the advice of the police should be sought. The police can advise on likely criminal and security issues, and patterns of behaviour, thus providing an understanding of the local crime context. The police may also give advice on possible design solutions. It may be helpful to consider these proposals alongside advice from access groups and consultants, as well as other qualified design specialists, to ensure that solutions are accessible as well as secure.

Designing for community safety can draw on two methods for understanding the local crime context. *Crime pattern analysis* helps ensure that crime reduction-based planning measures are based upon a clear understanding of the local situation, avoiding making assumptions about the problems and their causes. *Crime risk assessment* allows planners to work closely with the police to identify the crime risks in specific locations and work out how they may be reduced.

Safer Places, the government's good practice guidance on crime prevention through the planning system, sets out the seven attributes that contribute to making places both safe and sustainable. These are:

1. Access and movement

Places with well-defined routes, spaces and entrances that provide for convenient movement without compromising security.

2. Structure

Places that are structured, so that different uses do not cause conflict.

3. Surveillance

Places where all publicly accessible spaces are overlooked.

4. Ownership

Places that promote a sense of ownership, respect, territorial responsibility and community.

5. Physical protection

Places that include necessary, well-designed, security features.

6. Activity

Places where the level of human activity is appropriate to the location, and creates a reduced risk of crime and a sense of safety at all times.

7. Management and maintenance

Places that are designed with management and maintenance in mind, to discourage crime in the present and the future.

Environmental impact

These days, ever-higher standards of environmental protection and resource management are required. It is not just a matter of introducing simple mitigation measures, such as erecting a noise barrier or flood wall, planting trees to screen a view, or providing bat boxes. Environmental measures will influence the amount, layout, scale, design and appearance of the development.

The design statement should show how matters of environmental impact have shaped the design. Such matters will include:

- Flood control

- Water resource management

Indicative masterplan for the former Akzo Nobel Site in Littleborough by Taylor Young and Woodford Land

- Pollution control

- Conserving and enhancing landscape and townscape character

- Landscape screening

- Energy generation and conservation

- Minimising waste

- Attenuating noise

- Protecting nature and creating habitats

- Protecting and enhancing historic features.

What form should the design statement take?

The detail and scope of a design statement should match the size, sensitivity and complexity of the project. The design statement for a major development will need to be detailed and comprehensive. That for a simple householder application may need to be only a page or two.

Every design statement should include, as a minimum:

- A short, illustrated statement setting out the site and context appraisal, the purpose of the proposed development, a list of design principles, and a description of the proposal explaining how the design responds to the appraisal and design principles.

- A plan showing the site, the surrounding built or natural form, and key features identified in the appraisal.

- Annotated sketches and photographs to illustrate important elements of the context that inform the design principles.

- Plans and elevations of the proposal.

39

Except for householder applications, every design statement should include:

■ A short, written statement to show how the design responds to government guidance (including planning policy statements), regional planning guidance, the local development framework, any supplementary planning documents, urban design frameworks, local design guides and development briefs. (To avoid overloading the design statement, it may be appropriate sometimes to describe much of the planning policy background in a *planning statement*, to which the design statement should refer.)

■ A short statement on how the principles of inclusive design will be followed, including standards used, consultations to be undertaken and use of any access consultants.

■ An explanation of how the design statement will be updated through the decision-making process.

One approach is to refer to the structure set out in *By Design*, and explain how the proposals will achieve the seven objectives of urban design. (The Checklist on p-56 suggests how this can be done.) Each of the objectives should be referred to, even though not all of them will have equal weight in all projects.

For more complex and large-scale projects, it may be appropriate for the design statement to include:

a) *Site analysis*

■ Detailed analysis of the site, adjoining built or natural form and wider townscape/landscape. Detailed surveys may be required to ensure that adequate information has been obtained as a basis for design solutions. English Heritage's character assessment approach may be appropriate.

■ A review of environmental effects for projects that do not require an environmental statement (ES) under the Town and Country Planning (Environmental Impact Assessment)(England and Wales) Regulations 1999. An EIA will help to identify, early in the design process, those environmental issues that need to be attended to.

Design concept diagrams from the design statement for St Andrew Square, Edinburgh, by Comprehensive Design Architects for Coal Pension Properties.

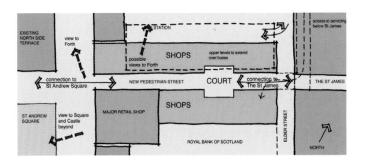

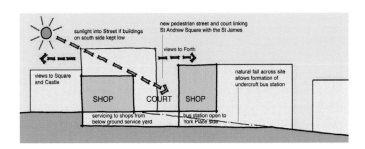

b) Design principles

- Urban/landscape design concept drawings to illustrate how the development will be integrated into the surrounding townscape and landscape.

- A description of the project's design principles.

- A report of any consultations undertaken.

- An outline of the feasibility evaluation and design stages carried out; identification of the design team; and any important design issues.

c) Conceptual design solutions

- Coloured plans of the proposals to illustrate the relationship between the existing features and the design.

- Site sections at a large scale through the development; medium sections to illustrate the relationship between the site, the proposals and the wider surroundings; and long sections to illustrate views.

- Sketches, photomontages and computer-generated visual simulations.

- An explanation of how the inclusive design principles have been translated into the design.

For larger or more sensitive developments, the design statement might usefully include:

- A programme of meetings with the local authority and other bodies.

- A programme of access and community consultations.

- A summary of any pre-application consultations undertaken. Explain who, what and where; what comments were received; and how the design evolved in response to the consultations.

- A short summary in clear, jargon-free English that could also be used to inform the public and the press, and which can be made available in alternative formats for disabled people.

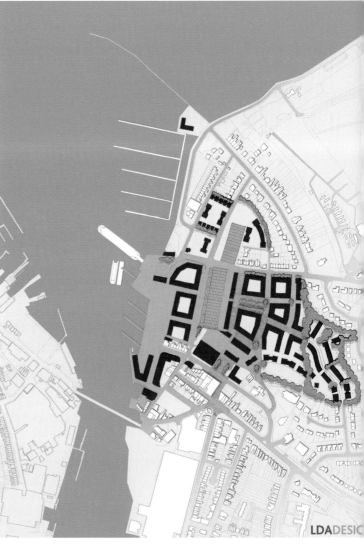

Three development options illustrated in the design statement by LDA Design for development at East Cowes. Many design statements neglect to set out options, but explaining how the options were prepared, evaluated and selected can be a useful aid to understanding a development proposal.

For very large and complex proposals that may have very specific impacts and design requirements, the applicant should discuss and agree additional design information with the council.

Options

Developers should be encouraged to explain in the design statement how they developed their design options, and how they chose the last one. Unfortunately developers often find it difficult to be open about the design options they have considered. They may be worried that the local authority will favour an option that they themselves have rejected.

Format of the document

The design statement should normally be A4 size in portrait format or A3 size in landscape format. It is acceptable to submit a design statement electronically, unless the local planning authority specifically requires a hard copy. CDs should be submitted

42

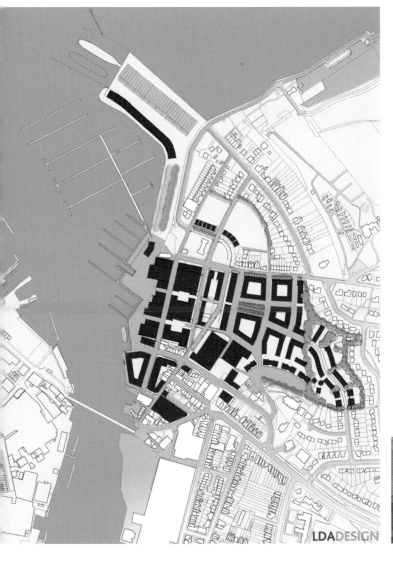

The statement should be easily legible.

where local authorities have the appropriate technology, in line with e-government policy to move towards web-based planning registers. Applicants should contact the local authority to find out which format will ensure that councillors and the public will be able to see the design statement.

The statement should be easily legible and reproducible. Reviewing and updating it should be straightforward.

The templates and checklists provided by Manchester Disabled People's Access Group include prompts for accessible elements, and applicants and planners can use them as a record.

43

Part Three
Procedures for decision-making

Part Three
Procedures for decision-making

Using design statements in assessing planning applications

How design statements relate to the planning and design process

THE PLANNING AND DESIGN PROCESS	THE DESIGN STATEMENT
The client assembles a project team	**Preliminary discussions between the project team and local authority**
The local authority confirms the need for a design statement and its requirements (as appropriate)	**The project team and local authority agree the contents and requirements of the design statement**
The project team charts the process of the design statement	**The project team and local authority agree the programme for preparing the design statement**
The project team charts its approach to the design statement	**The project team and local authority agree approaches to context appraisal, community engagement, design principles and placemaking**
The local authority maintains a watching brief over the design process	**The project team undertakes the activities agreed with the local authority**
The design statement is submitted as part of either an outline or full planning application	**The local authority carries out a comprehensive assessment of the application and design statement**

How design statements relate to application type

TYPE OF APPLICATION	MEANS OF FIXING THE DESIGN STATEMENT
Outline planning application	**Conditions and reserved matters based on elements identified in the design statement**
Full planning application or listed building consent application	**Conditions based on elements identified in the design statement**

46

The applicant should find out who needs to be consulted, and carry out the appropriate consultations accordingly. Applicants are encouraged to consult the local authority at an early stage. The council should respond constructively, giving a clear indication of its expectations. It will also carry out its own consultations. For major projects, the local authority may be able to help the applicant consult other parties with an interest in the design aspects of the proposal. Such parties may include local civic societies, a local design panel, the local authority's design 'champion', parish councils, CABE, English Heritage, or a regional development agency's design panel.

An initial discussion with the local authority to decide the scope of the design statement will help the applicant to identify at an early stage what should be included in surveys and assessments; the level of detail and rigour to such analysis; whether third-party experts need to be commissioned; who needs to be consulted; and what may be appropriate as design principles. This may form the first stage of pre-application discussions with the council.

Agreeing the contents and level of detail required at the outset should reduce the need to submit supplementary information, often at greater cost and leading to design revisions. It will also help to avoid unnecessary expense in smaller projects.

Once satisfied that the design statement meets the relevant requirements, the local planning authority should place it on the public register with the application to which it relates. The statement should also be sent with the planning application to people who are being formally consulted.

The design statement should accompany the planning application and ES or other submission, if required. Local planning authorities may stipulate that planning applications will not be registered until all the submission requirements have been met. The lack of a design statement may lead to delay. It may be possible to submit supplementary information, such as photomontages, at a later stage, but local planning authorities will be able to deal with applications more quickly if all design material is submitted together.

The council should tell applicants if it feels that their intentions and its policies are fundamentally incompatible. Applicants who still wish to proceed with the application should be aware that the preparation of a design statement and any other work undertaken to present the proposal will be at their own risk.

The council may make use of planning conditions and planning obligations to secure a high quality of design. In assessing submissions in relation to these, it will expect the detailed design to comply with the principles of the previously submitted design statement unless subsequent changes can be justified.

Changes may be justified in the following circumstances:

- The discovery of significant new information that was not available at the time of preparing the design statement.

- Further consultations having been held with disabled people and members of local communities or specialist groups.

- Changes in government policy or guidance since the time of the original application.

- Material economic changes or advances in technology, provided that these do not introduce substantial new environmental or design considerations (in which case a revised design statement may be required).

- The publication of new studies or advice that affect existing circumstances, such as village design statements or conservation area appraisals.

- The adoption of new development plans affecting the proposal, including those in adjoining districts.

The council will refer back to the principles underlying the design statement when it considers any subsequent application for changes or resolution of conditions or matters of detail.

47

The council will reject any poor designs, in particular where the design is contrary to local plan policy, supplementary planning documents (SPDs), or adopted landscape, urban design and management guidelines. Designs will be considered poor where they fail to respect and respond to their context and surroundings, fail to respond well to site conditions, or fail to meet agreed design principles. It is hoped that the use of design statements will help to ensure that bad proposals are rare, and that such schemes will generally be aborted prior to any application being submitted.

Design statements are one of the main tools used in assessing planning applications, as routine as the submission of forms, site plans, plans and elevations.

Local authority procedures

A local planning authority will need to agree procedures on, among others, the following matters:

- Deciding whether the design statement is adequate for the planning application to be registered.

- Deciding whether the design statement provides the information required or if further information is needed.

- Deciding whether or not to charge a fee for pre-application discussions.

- Deciding how decision-makers are to be made aware of and helped to understand design statements, their principles and explanations.

- Explaining in the local development framework how design statements will be used.

Using design statements in assessing planning applications

Points for development control planners to consider:

- Read the design statement thoroughly.

- Do not assume that it is a good design statement just because it is big and glossy.

- Do not assess the application's drawings without first reading the design statement.

- Do not accept the design statement just because the design of the scheme looks acceptable.

- Do not allow the subjective views of council officers and members to cloud a clearly argued design rationale based on careful analysis of the context.

- Use checklists to ensure consistency.

- Be clear about the level of accessibility required and standards used.

- Be clear about the amount of consultation which should take place.

Other types of statement

A wide variety of other kinds of statements and documents may also relate to the planning proposal. These may include statements, surveys and reports on biodiversity, ecology, archaeology, trees or the use of sustainable energy and renewable resources, for example. The design statement should avoid repetition as much as possible; it should be clear how the documents relate to one another and should be cross-referenced.

Planning statements

A planning statement is a full record of the planning policies relevant to a particular site and its planning history. Such a statement may be prepared by a planning authority or developer for a variety of reasons. The existence of a planning statement does not make a design statement any less necessary. The design statement is likely to cover some of the same ground (although probably in less detail) as well as many other matters.

Environmental statements

A planning application may also require an environmental statement, under the Town and Country Planning (Environmental Impact Assessment)(England and Wales) Regulations 1999, to accompany the design statement. The information contained in the environmental statement should not be duplicated in the design statement, so careful presentation of the relevant information for each statement will be needed, with appropriate cross-references. However, the design statement should show how design considerations arising from the environmental statement have been taken account of in the design process.

A diagram of the layout of existing buildings from the design statement for a sustainable neighbourhood at Holton Heath by Roger Evans Associates (REAL) for BL Holdings, David Wilson Estates and the Secretary of State for Defence.

Environmental impact

Few planning applications require an environmental statement. Many more will either require, or the applicant will volunteer, a review of environmental effects. This can modify the development and its design, rather than just leading to finding ways to mitigate its impact. The aim is to achieve a good design, not just a technical fix. That may require the input of a range of specialists: design is more than just architecture and urban design. If the environmental review does lead to the design being modified, the changes should be incorporated into the design statement.

Transport and travel plans

Although transport and travel plans can have a major impact on planning and the design of development, they are often undertaken independently of the design and planning processes. It is important for design statements to refer to them where appropriate and take account of design issues arising from the preparation of the plans, including any impact on access for disabled people.

Professional advice

A range of professionals is available to help planning applicants prepare design statements and design development, including urban designers, architects, landscape architects, highway engineers, access consultants and town planners. A great deal depends on selecting the right advisors and consultants, and managing them effectively. With major projects it is important to ensure adequate continuity of advisors throughout what may be a long design, planning and development process.

49

Tricks of the trade

Some applicants misuse the planning process. Their tricks of the trade threaten to bring the process into disrepute. Applicants who want to build a constructive relationship with the local authority will avoid these tricks, and local authorities committed to higher standards of design will not be taken in by them. Achieving the potential that design statements offer depends on both applicants and local planning authorities adopting better practice.

1. Trick of the trade: responding to local context

What the design statement says:

'The area's characteristic style is of predominantly half-timbered housing.'

What the applicant really means:

'There are a couple of half-timbered houses in an adjoining street, and it just happens that one of our standard house types has a half-timbered look.'

50

2. Trick of the trade: the confidence trick

What the design statement says:

'The proposal was drawn up in close consultation with the council's planners and highway engineers, who expressed their support at every stage.'

What the applicant really means:

'They kept telling us our ideas were rubbish but we ignored them.'

3. Trick of the trade: how to illustrate a design statement

Include photographs of Venice to show what your development will look like, more or less (without the sunshine, the medieval architecture and the water, of course).

51

4. Trick of the trade: how to save on design costs

a) Hire a competent architect to draw up a scheme and to write the design statement. This will impress the planners.

b) Get planning permission on the basis of that impressive application.

c) Ditch the architect.

d) Get your technician or a design-and-build outfit to draw up a cheaper scheme.

e) Submit a further planning application, similar enough to the previous one, to make it hard for the local authority to refuse, but lacking all the design quality.

5. Trick of the trade: designing tall buildings

a) **Even if whoever designed the scheme has never visited the site, say in the design statement that the scheme has been designed in response to its surroundings.**

b) **If it's ridiculously out of scale with its surroundings, call it a landmark.**

c) **If anyone asks what it's a landmark to, call it an icon.**

6.   Trick of the trade: just a minute

a)   Arrange a meeting with the planners. Send them the minutes of the meeting, creating a totally erroneous record of what the planners said.

b)   With luck, the planners will be too busy to read the minutes carefully and will fail to challenge them.

c)   The minutes can later be quoted at a public inquiry to support the applicant's assertion that the council's rejection of the proposal came out of the blue.

7. Trick of the trade: bamboozling the planners

a) Pester the planners for meetings, turn up at the council offices to see them, and phone them as often as possible.

b) Include a record of these contacts in the design statement as evidence of how the development proposal was drawn up in close collaboration with the planners, whose refusal of the application can then be said at the public inquiry to have been an unexpected bolt from the blue.

8.   Trick of the trade: the back-to-front design statement

a)   Draw the development scheme on the back of an envelope in a flash of inspiration in the pub.

b)   Invent a set of design principles that look as though they would have led to the design you came up with, and describe them in a design statement.

c)   Explain in the design statement how those principles were derived from analysing the site (even though they were not).

Part Four
Checklist for preparing a design and access statement

Using the checklist

This checklist presents an outline of matters that might be covered by a design statement (or, in the CLG's current phrase, a design and access statement). Which of them will be included, and in what detail, will depend on the site, its context, and the nature of the proposed development. It is not a compulsory list of contents.

A design statement is an aid to communication. Excessive, inappropriate detail will cause confusion. In the case of a very small development proposal, the design statement may fit onto one page. For a more complex scheme it may be a substantial document. The local authority will advise on what the design statement should include and what level of detail will be appropriate.

Many design statements contain large amounts of text that convey very little. The following extensive checklist is provided to help applicants produce design statements that are well structured but as concise as possible. In any particular case many of the categories may not be relevant, and many others may be capable of being answered in a few words, or through illustrations. A picture can be worth a thousand words (unless it is a misleading marketing graphic) and ten well-chosen words are worth ten pages of jargon.

A design statement accompanies a planning application, so there is no need for it to repeat what is in the application itself. The statement's purpose is to help the design to develop and to explain and justify the application.

A design statement should generally include the following sections:

1. Background

2. Policy summary

3. Consultations and advice

4. Site and context appraisal

5. Rationale

6. Design principles (including access standards used)

7. Options

8. The scheme.

Too often a design statement includes a detailed description of the development's internal organisation, a schedule of room sizes and so on. Such material should be excluded unless there is a good reason for including it.

The function of a design statement is very different to that of an architect's report to a client, or to a developer's marketing material. The statement should be written for an audience of planning officers, planning committees and members of the local community who are interested or who are being consulted.

A design statement is part of the planning process. The aspects of design that are relevant to the planning system are set out in *By Design* and in Circular 01/06 (CLG). The most important job of a design statement is to explain what design principles the proposal is based on, how they are derived from the context, and how those principles have shaped the design.

The information provided in the design statement can also be used as part of the information provided for access statements required for building control approval. Some planning authorities require additional information at planning stage, including internal specifications, particularly with regard to listed buildings.

Note

This checklist follows a similar structure to that set out in the Urban Design Group's guide *Urban Design Guidance: urban design frameworks, development briefs and master plans*. This is because many of the basic elements of a design statement are the same as those of an urban design guidance document, and because both checklists follow the structure recommended in the CLG/CABE guidance, *By Design*. This present checklist has been tailored for design statements and updated.

A representation of a proposal by Savills at Featherstone, South Staffordshire, for Taylor Wimpey

59

1. Background

The site

What are the boundaries of the site?

■ Include references to site and location plans.

Date

When was the design statement prepared?

Proposed uses

What land uses are proposed?

■ preferred

■ acceptable

■ unacceptable.

2. Policy summary

What policies and guidance of the local planning authority or other public bodies apply, and how will they be interpreted in relation to this site?

The local authority may request a full policy review to be provided in a document called a *planning statement*. It will usually be appropriate for the design statement to list this material in a concise *policy summary*. Such a summary may need to take account of (but not describe in full) the following.

Local authority planning policies

Which of the local authority's planning policies apply to the site?

Refer to the relevant policies but do not quote them at length. Make contact with relevant parts of the local authority beyond development control, if appropriate, to discuss the impact of the proposed development on the local authority's wider objectives. The council should be able to help facilitate such contacts and present a coherent approach.

Relevant policies may cover, among other things:

■ access standards and guidance

■ airport protection zones

■ ancient monuments

■ archaeology

■ conservation areas

■ design

■ economic development

■ education

■ environmental health

■ high buildings

■ highways

- housing
- interim uses
- land uses
- landscape and amenity space
- leisure
- listed buildings
- local nature reserves and other designated ecological sites
- nature conservation, countryside and green strategies
- materials
- parking
- protected flora and fauna
- public realm
- public transport
- renewable energy
- shopping (retail)
- sites of special scientific interest
- social services
- street design
- strategic and local views
- town centres.

Other local authority policies and standards

Are other local authority policies or standards relevant to development here?

Planning and design guidance

Is the site covered by a design guide, an urban design framework, a development brief, a masterplan, access standards, or any other supplementary planning guidance?

Local design statement

Is the area covered by a local design statement (a document explaining what aspects of the physical form of an area local people value and the design principles on which they hope future development will be based)?

Landscape, townscape and character appraisals

Have any landscape, townscape or character appraisals been carried out for the site or area?

Conservation areas and listed buildings

Is the site in or near a conservation area? Is it covered by a conservation area statement, a conservation plan or any appraisals? If so, how have these been integrated into or referred to in the design statement? Are there listed building on or near the site?

61

Planning history of the site, including previous planning decisions and results of public consultations

What planning documents are relevant to the site? What previous planning decisions need to be taken into account? Have any public consultations been carried out in relation to the area or site? If so, what were the results?

3. Consultations and advice

What consultations have been carried out and what advice has been received from specialist and expert organisations and individuals?

4. Site and context appraisal

What aspects of the place have been taken into account in drawing up the design principles and designing the scheme?

Plans and illustrations for the appraisal

What plans are appropriate for a design statement will depend on the scale and complexity of the site and its setting. It is essential to establish from what and where the context and cues for design are derived. A design statement should always contain the following plan:

■ Location plan, with north point, scale and Ordnance Survey grid reference.

■ Plans of site and surrounding area, with north points, indication of scale of plans, and contours or levels.

The following may be appropriate:

a) Historic plans, where these provide useful information about how the area has developed.

b) Figure/ground diagrams can be a useful way of showing the relationship between built form and publicly accessible space (including streets) by presenting the former in black and the latter as a white background (or the other way around).

c) Photographs (including aerial).

d) Drawings (including sections through the site and streets).

e) Historic drawings and photographs.

f) Context appraisal diagrams (annotated diagrams showing the significance of various features of the area, summarising what the area appraisal describes in greater detail).

g) Public realm appraisal diagrams.

h) Space syntax analysis diagrams to assess the spatial integration of routes, and pedestrian flows.

Written appraisal

The written appraisal with illustrations will describe the features of the area that are likely to be relevant to development. This should be brief. Bullet points are to be preferred over extensive text.

Access audits and reports

Where an access audit has recently been carried out for a building, or an organisation has a record of complaints or difficulties, these can highlight barriers to access and ways of overcoming them.

62

Land ownership

How is the site's ownership divided? Who are the owners?

Land uses

What is the site used for at present (including informal uses)?

What uses are found in the surrounding area?

In what ways are the existing uses likely to be sensitive to how the place is developed?

Development capacity

What indications are there of how much development the place is likely to be able to accommodate? Are these justified by the design direction taken?

Appraising the site and area in terms of urban design objectives

By Design (CLG/CABE) identifies seven objectives of urban design (character; continuity and enclosure; convivial public realm; ease of movement; legibility; adaptability; and diversity). These objectives can be used to structure a site and context appraisal, and they provide headings to the following checklist. Additional matters of integration and efficiency have been included in the checklist to focus on the degree to which the proposed development is likely to be sustainable.

Character

NATURAL FEATURES

Landscape setting and type	What sort of landscape does the place have?
Land form	What is the shape of the land?
	Where does it rise and fall?
Hydrology	Where is there water and how does it move (including rivers, streams, lakes, ponds and swampy or floodable ground)?
Geology and soils	What are the soils, sub-soils and rocks?
Ecology and wildlife	What living things (flora and fauna) are to be found on the site and in the area?
	What do they depend on?
Trees and hedgerows	What trees and hedgerows are to be found here?
	■ Location
	■ Species
	■ Condition
	■ Size
	■ Tree preservation orders
Climate	What sort of climate does the area have and what changes can be expected?
	What are the prevailing winds in summer and winter?

63

Microclimate	What is the climate like in the area (and in particular parts of it)? For example: ■ Exposure to wind and weather ■ Wind funnels ■ Cold air drainage channels ■ Frost pockets ■ Damp hollows.
Orientation	Which way does the site (or parts of it) slope or face in relation to the sun?

HUMAN IMPACT

Boundaries	What are the boundaries of the site?
Area	What is the area of the site in hectares?
Contamination	Is the ground contaminated? What would be involved in cleaning it up?
Pollution	Is the air or water polluted? What would be involved in purifying it?
Undermining	Has the site been undermined?
Aesthetic quality	What are the site's most visually attractive features?
Noise	Do any parts of the site suffer from noise? What would be involved in alleviating it?
Historical development	How did the site develop in the past?
Settlement pattern	What sort of street layout does the area have?
Archaeology	Do any sites need to be investigated (through records or by digging) for possible archaeological value?
Cultural characteristics and heritage	What is distinctive about the way local people live and have lived here in the past?
Local history	What aspects of local history may be relevant to future development?
Events/festivals	What local events and festivals will be taken account of in planning and designing in the area?
Census data	What information from the census will be taken account of in planning and designing in the area?

BUILDINGS AND STRUCTURES

Colour and textures	What distinctive colours and textures are found on buildings, structures and surfaces in the area?
Facade treatments	What distinctive types of building front are there in the area?
Building elements and fenestration	What locally distinctive ways are there of using elements of a building such as windows, doors, cornices, string courses, bargeboards, porches and chimneys?

Rhythm and pattern	What regularity and order does the streetscape have?
Details and richness	How are building details and materials used to contribute to the area's interest?
Local/regional building materials	What building materials are used traditionally in the area, and which materials are available in the region?
Local vernacular	In what other traditional ways do or did local builders work?
Age of built fabric	What are the ages of buildings and structures in the area?
Listed buildings	Are any buildings or structures statutorily or locally listed for their architectural or historical value?

CONTINUITY AND ENCLOSURE

Continuity	Are the building lines continuous, or do gap sites and abnormal setbacks interrupt them?
Enclosure	How do buildings, structures and natural features contribute to or detract from a feeling of enclosure?
Back views	Do any buildings present their backs to public space, including roads?
Active frontages	Are frontages at ground floor level active or dead?

CONVIVIAL PUBLIC REALM

Connected routes	How is the site connected into the network of streets?
Overlooking	Are public routes and spaces overlooked, making them safer?
Hard landscape	What is the character and materials of paving, kerbs, walls, steps and ramps?
Planting	What trees, planters and grassed or planted areas are there?
Street furniture	What signs, seats, bins, bollards, manhole covers, tree grilles and railings are there? Are they protected in ways that are convenient for disabled people?
Structures	What bus shelters, kiosks, stalls, information points, pedestrian bridges, beacons and temporary structures are there?
Safety and security	What safety and security facilities (such as closed circuit television) are there?
Maintenance	How easy are publicly accessible places to maintain?
Landscape	Is the landscape included in the Register of Historic Parks and Gardens or a local inventory?

EASE OF MOVEMENT

Public transport	What public transport routes and stops serve the area?
Roads	What is the area's road network?

65

Access	What are the present and potential means of getting to and around the area for vehicles (including bicycles, cars and service vehicles) and pedestrians (including disabled people – not just wheelchair and buggy users, but also visually impaired people, deaf people, learning disabled people and others)? Are there any access barriers, obstructions or hazards, or places where there should be features such as dropped kerbs or controlled crossings?
Parking and drop-off	What parking and drop-off arrangements are there, including appropriate accessible parking for disabled people?
	Is the site within a controlled parking zone?
Pedestrian routes and flows	Where do people travel, walk on, to or near here? What routes would they like to take if they were available? Are there any steep gradients that would be barriers for disabled people?
Traffic and pedestrians	How do traffic and pedestrians interact? Are there places where they share space? Do disabled people face hazards?
Cycling	What facilities for cycling are there?
Transport proposals	What current proposals for roads, footpaths or public transport might be relevant to future development?
Transport assessment	Will a transport assessment be required?
Travel plans	Will a green travel plan be required?
Air quality	How does the air quality influence movement choices?

LEGIBILITY (EASE OF UNDERSTANDING)

Image and perception	What image, if any, do people (locals and outsiders) have of the place?
Local views	What is visible from particular points in or around the area?
Strategic views	What is visible from particular distant points, and what distant views are there?
Vistas	Are there any notable narrow views past a series of landmarks?
Landmarks	What buildings or structures (on or visible from here) stand out from the background buildings?
Skylines	What buildings (on or visible from here) can be seen against the sky?
Roofscape	What sort of views of roofs are there from (and of) the place?
Gateways	Are there places at the edge of the area or site that are seen (or could potentially be seen) as gateways to it?
Thresholds	Are there places at the edge of (or within) the area or site that are seen (or could potentially be seen) as points where its function or character (or development on it) changes?
Boundaries and barriers	What boundaries and barriers are there at the edge of (or within) the area or site?
Nodes	Are there points (nodes) where activity is concentrated and routes intersect?

66

ADAPTABILITY

What aspects of the site and its existing buildings contribute to the ability to reuse existing structures or features, or to the future adaptability of the proposed development?

DIVERSITY

What aspects of the area or site and its existing buildings contribute to their potential for choice and diversity, including – if appropriate – a mix of uses?

Do the proposed uses conform to the adopted development plan or local development framework, or would they represent a departure from the development plan?

INTEGRATION AND EFFICIENCY

What is the area's carrying capacity (its ability to support development or human activities without unacceptable consequences)?

What aspects of the area or site and its existing buildings contribute to its potential for using energy and other resources efficiently?

Solar energy	What opportunities are there for development to make use of daylight, solar gain, solar panels or photovoltaic technology?
Underground energy	What opportunities are there for making use of underground energy sources, by means of heat pumps?
Water	What opportunities are there for reducing water run-off and flood risk, and recycling water?
	What opportunities are there for using aquifers to cool buildings?
	What opportunities are there for sustainable urban drainage systems (SUDs)?
Wind	How can the wind be used for ventilation and as an energy source?
Waste	How can the use of non-renewable resources (including energy, land, water and building materials) be minimised?

Does the area or site offer any other opportunities for integrating land use, transport and the natural environment (including minimising journeys by car and maximising the use of public transport)?

5. Rationale

How did the analysis of the context lead to the chosen design principles?

This section need not be long. A simple explanation is all that is needed. But it is the essential link between the site and context appraisal and the design principles.

67

6. Design principles

What design principles and access standards have been or will be followed in developing the site?

Design concept

What is the central idea on which the design is based?

What is the vision of the potential of the site and surrounding area?

Mix of uses

How will a mix of uses be achieved?

Proposed disposition of uses

How will the uses be arranged in the area or on the site?

Features to be retained

Which of the area's buildings or landscape features will be kept? How have they influenced the design options?

The form of new development

By Design (CLG/CABE) identifies eight aspects of development form. These are urban structure; urban grain; landscape; density and mix; height; massing; details; and materials. (Urban structure and urban grain are aspects of layout; height and massing are aspects of scale; and details and materials are aspects of appearance.) The design statement should describe how the proposed development form will help achieve the seven objectives of urban design identified by *By Design* (character; continuity and enclosure; quality of the public realm; ease of movement; legibility; adaptability; and diversity).

Layout: urban structure	How will buildings, routes and open spaces be placed in relation to each other (in two dimensions)? How will they relate to their townscape and landscape settings?
	How will routes and spaces connect to the local area and more widely?
Layout: urban grain	How will the area's pattern of blocks and plot subdivisions be arranged?
	Where will building entrances be positioned? How will they be identified easily?
	How will buildings (particularly their windows, active frontages and doors) relate to the public realm?
Density	What mass or floorspace of a building or buildings will be provided?
	How do the densities relate to the area's carrying capacity (its ability to support development or human activities without unacceptable consequences)?
	The density of a development can be expressed in terms of:
	■ its plot ratio (for commercial development)

68

■ the number of habitable rooms per hectare (for residential development)

■ the area of site covered plus the number of floors or a maximum building height

■ space standards

■ a combination of the above.

Height	What will be the height of buildings and structures?

The following matters should be among those considered in deciding on appropriate heights:

■ the relationship between buildings and spaces

■ the visual impact of the development on views, vistas and skylines.

The height of a building can be expressed in terms of:

■ a maximum number of floors

■ a maximum height of parapet or ridge

■ a maximum overall height

■ any of these maximum heights in combination with a maximum number of floors

■ a ratio of building height to street or space width

■ height relative to particular landmarks or background buildings

■ strategic views. |
| *Massing* | How will the buildings or groups of buildings be arranged in three dimensions (shape and volume)? |
| *Details* | What principles will be followed in designing the details of buildings, structures and spaces here?

Details include:

■ craftsmanship

■ building techniques

■ facade treatment

■ lighting

■ accessibility issues. |
| *Materials* | What principles will be followed in selecting the materials for buildings, structures and spaces?

Relevant aspects of materials include:

■ texture (including ensuring that there are no hazards for people with visual impairments)

■ colour (including luminance and colour contrast)

■ pattern (including avoiding confusing patterns for people with visual impairments and learning difficulties)

■ durability

■ ease of maintenance

■ smooth surfaces for people with mobility impairments. |

69

Landscape and open space design

Structure planting	Where will new planting (including shrubs, trees and hedges) be provided to contribute to the basic form of the development? Will it avoid creating visual or transport barriers for disabled people?
Secondary planting	Where will other new planting be provided?
Species choice	What species will be appropriate? Will the interests of visually impaired people be considered (in relation to scent and touch, for example)?
Hard landscape	What hard landscape (including paving and boundaries) will be created?
Public space	What public space will be provided and how will it be treated?
Private open space	What private open space is provided and how is its amenity maximised?
Enclosure	How will spaces (public and private) be enclosed?
Character	What will be the character of the open spaces?
Lighting	How will the spaces be lit? Will undesirable glare and shadows be avoided?

Movement

Access to site	How will vehicle and pedestrian access be provided?
Access to public transport	How will access to public transport be provided?
Network of roads, footpaths and cycleways	How will a connected network of roads, footpaths and cycleways be provided?
Accessibility for disabled people	How will the site be made fully accessible to as many people people as possible (including people with sensory and neuro-diverse impairments, learning disabled people and people with mobility impairments, and for other users, such as older people and parents with children)?
Traffic management	What principles will apply to traffic management here?
Parking	How will parking (including designated accessible parking) be provided?
	Is a statement required that the future occupants of the development be excluded from applying for a residents' parking permit?

Safety

Are there any additional ways in which development will contribute to making the place safe?

Security

Are there any additional ways in which the development will contribute to making property secure?

Energy

How will the development make use of solar energy (daylight, solar gain, solar panels and photovoltaic technology)?

How will the potential for combined heat and power or cogeneration be made use of?

How will the potential for energy generation by biomass (plant material grown for purpose or wood waste) be made use of?

How will the potential for wind power be made use of?

How will the potential for ground source energy be made use of?

What opportunities are there for using aquifers to cool buildings?

Water

How will the development reduce water run-off, minimise flood risk and recycle water?

Waste

How will the collection and separation of waste be facilitated through, among other things, the design of bin stores and refuse vehicle routes?

Microclimate

How will summer cooling and shade be provided?

How will the landscape be used to modify temperature?

How will the landscape and materials be used to moderate humidity?

How will planting on roofs and walls maximise transpiration?

How will the design of the landscape avoid frost pockets?

Public art

How will public art be used?

Management and maintenance

How will the development be managed and maintained?

Illustrating the design principles and the proposed approach

Depending on the size and complexity of the proposed development, it may be appropriate to include:

Concept diagrams	Diagrams showing the basic principles on which the form of new development will be based.
Building envelope guidelines	Diagrams with dimensions, showing the possible site and massing of a building.
Indicative sketches	Drawings indicating building forms and spaces.
Axonometric drawings	At 1:500 scale.
Photographs, drawings and case studies	Showing and describing other examples, locally or elsewhere. Use overseas examples with care: they may make it harder for some people to understand how the scheme works in practice and may encourage some that the design would not be appropriate in the UK.

71

Urban design strategy diagram	
Diagrams	Showing such features as the impact on the light (and other aspects of the amenity) of adjoining buildings.
Illustrations	Showing a palette of materials.
An accurate visual representation (AVR)	A picture showing a proposed building or structure alongside what already exists, for use in evaluating a development proposal. Types of AVR include:

- *Visibility study* (a simple depiction of the shape of a proposal shown on digital photographs).

- *Approximate photomontage* (a rendered computer model of a proposed building or structure combined with a photograph of its surroundings).

- *Accurate silhouette* (an accurate description of the position, shape and size of a proposal, shown on a high-resolution photograph).

- *Accurate photomontage* (an accurate depiction of the position, shape and size of a proposal but with selected architectural details shown on a high-resolution photograph).

- *Accurate photo-reality* (an accurate depiction of the position, size, shape and external appearance of a development proposal).

The design statement should not include seductive marketing images. These will only serve to reduce its credibility.

7. Options

What options were considered, what consultations were undertaken, and how and why was the chosen option selected?

8. The scheme

Government guidance says that a design statement should explain the design principles and concepts that have been applied to particular aspects of the proposal in terms of the amount, layout, scale, landscaping and appearance of the development, and the access implications of these. Some local planning authorities insist on these specific terms being used to structure any design statement, so be sure to mention them prominently, and provide clear cross-referencing so that a reader can find the relevant information in the design statement (particularly in the section on design principles).

The design statement should explain how the final scheme responds to the design principles that were set out earlier in the design statement.

Urban Design Group
Membership Application Form

Name

Delivery address

Postcode

Telephone

Mobile

Fax

Email

Billing address (if different)

Course/Year (students only)

Current membership of professional institutes

Employer's name

Address

Postcode

Telephone

Email

Indicate the region to which you wish to be affiliated (tick one only):

East Midlands ❏ West Midlands ❏ East Anglia ❏ North ❏
North East ❏ North West ❏ South West ❏ South ❏
Yorkshire ❏ London and SE ❏ Scotland ❏ Wales ❏
Northern Ireland ❏ Outside UK ❏

Please tick membership category

❏ Individual   £40
❏ Student/Concession £20 (UK only)
❏ Library   £40
❏ Local authority   £100 (includes two copies of UDQ)
❏ Practice   £250 (includes entries in UDQ
                         Practice Index and Sourcebook, and
                         listing on website)

Tick here if you do not want to receive mailings of job adverts ❏

Paying your subscription by standing order is a great help to the UDG

Details for Standing Order Mandate
(to be sent to UDG)

To (name of bank)

Bank address

Bank postcode

Bank sort code

Please pay Natwest, 68 Church Street, Lancaster LA1 1LN
(Sort Code 01 54 90)
For the credit of the Urban Design Group
(account number 89621271)

The sum of £

Amount in words

Account name

Account number

Commencing

and then every 12 months

Or send a cheque payable to: Urban Design Group

Return your completed application to:

Urban Design Group
70 Cowcross Street, London EC1M 6EJ
Tel: 020 7250 0892
Fax: 020 7250 0872
admin@udg.org.uk

Signed   Date

Gift Aid declaration As a registered charity, the UDG can reclaim tax on your annual subscription through the Gift Aid scheme – as long as you are a taxpayer and pay an amount of income tax or capital gains tax at least equal to the tax we reclaim (currently 28p for each £1 you give). Please sign the declaration below if you are a taxpayer. It will not cost you anything, but the UDG will receive from the Inland Revenue tax you have already paid.
I wish the Urban Design Group to treat as Gift Aid all membership subscriptions I have paid on or after the date of this declaration.

Signed   Date

You can cancel this declaration at any time by contacting the Urban Design Group.